Floorquilts!

Fabric Decoupaged Floorcloths—

No-Sew Fun

ELLEN HIGHSMITH SILVER

C&T PUBLISHING

Photo by Parsley Steinweiss

Text copyright © 2007 by Ellen Highsmith Silver

Artwork copyright © 2007 by C&T Publishing, Inc.

Publisher: Amy Marson

Editorial Director: Gailen Runge

Editor: Stacy Chamness

Technical Editors: Ellen Pahl and Nanette S. Zeller

Copyeditor/Proofreader: Wordfirm Inc.

Cover Designer: Christina Jarumay

Book Designer: Rose Sheifer-Wright

Production Coordinators: Joshua Mulks and Kerry Graham

Illustrator: Richard Sheppard

Photography by C&T Publishing, Inc., unless otherwise noted

Published by C&T Publishing, Inc., P.O. Box 1456, Lafayette, CA 94549

Library of Congress Cataloging-in-Publication Data

Silver, Ellen Highsmith,

 Floorquilts : fabric decoupaged floorcloths—no-sew fun / Ellen Highsmith Silver.

    p. cm.

  ISBN-13: 978-1-57120-426-4 (paper trade : alk. paper)

  ISBN-10: 1-57120-426-1 (paper trade : alk. paper)

 1. Painting. 2. Floor coverings. 3. Decoupage. I. Title.

 TT385.S485 2007

 745.7'23--dc22   2007001745

Printed in China

10 9 8 7 6 5 4 3 2 1

CONTENTS

Photo by Parsley Steinweiss

Dedication

There are two extremely unselfish people to whom I owe the existence of this book. It is nice to have this dedicated place to express my appreciation.

Nancy Rosenberger, after a successful career in the textile industry, realized her dream of owning a quilt shop. I was lucky to be there at the beginning and ride the waves of her talents and enthusiasm. I made a floorquilt for her Quilt Cottage after unpacking a particularly glorious shipment of Kaffe Fassett fabrics. The floorquilt was well received, and Nancy kept after me until I agreed to teach a class. After the success of that class, I agreed that a book should be written. Nancy gave me the time to write it, doing both her job and mine. Her strong belief in my idea—supported by her willingness to do the work of two very energetic people until the book was finished—convinced me that this was worth doing.

Even though my husband, Mitch, is creative and tolerant, he has learned to be selectively supportive of my crafty pursuits. Therefore, it was heartening when my floorquilts won his approval as they began showing up underfoot. But when he—who was in the final stages of writing his own book—literally stepped up to the plate (after plate, after plate) and took over dinners and dirty dishes, I felt great relief and true support. It's also worth noting that when our house became the floorquilt production zone, he good-naturedly hopscotched around floorquilts in various stages of production.

Fabrics have always played a happy role in my life.

I am awfully proud that these two special folks chose to invest their energy in my idea of a good time.

Acknowledgments

The following people have each played a part in the drama (or dramedy) of writing this book. I wish to thank them all for their gift of faith in my mission and good humor when required: Linda Bagby, Malene Barnett, Allen Barstow, Marjorie Lee Bevis, Doreen Birdsell, Marie Browning, Frank Cappiello Jr., Theresa Capuana, Stacy Chamness, Margaret Cusack, Pete Delin, Pat DeSantis, Marsha Edell, Nancy Ehrlich, Karen Farrel, Liz Alpert Fay, Emmie Goldenbaum, Kathy Goodman, Jan Grigsby, Rita Hatten, Halisha Hayworth, Mike Henes, Barbara Hicks, Mary Highsmith, Starch Highsmith, Dawn Hutchins, Kathi Jahnke, Marlys Klein, Gail Kohler, Ann Krier, Glenda Lallatin, Mary Ann Lico, Carol Miller, Kate Perri, Jane Pollak, Lindsey Pollak, Lauren Powell, Eileen Puleo, Mary Quinlan, Mary Reed, Robinette Robinson, Peter Rosenberger, Degen Sayer, Denyse Schmidt, Isabel Schoenfeld, Sue Schwartz, Perry Silver, Raymond Silver, Sylvia Silver, Sloane Silver, Carole Smyth, Parsley Steinweiss, Gwen Strayer, Suzanne StTherese, Julia Varca, Kirsten Walther, Hilary Ward, Lois Weitzner, Susan Werner, Laurette Young, and Tom Young.

Introduction

A class photo of students and their first floorquilts

Photo by Parsley Steinweiss

Fabrics have always played a happy role in my life. Growing up in a small textile town in North Carolina, I loved visiting the local mills and watching the cotton prints rolling through the various stages of production. On Saturdays, I would see farmers' wives come to town wearing dresses made from feed sacks similar to the ones stacked up at the Farmer's Exchange. I found something very agreeable about this thrifty example of fabric's multifunctionality.

The concept of using fabrics as an artistic medium, like paint or clay, drew me into quiltmaking, which still gives me such joy. I get lost in creating my own works and constantly celebrate the creativity of other artists who work with fabrics.

Floorquilts are the serendipitous result of loving both fabrics and dogs. Because of the occasional "accidents" of older dogs and the chewing stages of puppies, our area rugs were suffering undeserved abuses. While I was mulling it over, that light-bulb moment occurred, and my first floorquilt was born. It satisfied all my criteria. It was made with fabric, protected the floors, was durable (both accident and chew proof), and provided color and design for any room. That first *Flowering Irish Chain* floorquilt (page 42), made in 2002, is still alive and well.

I began teaching floorquilting because people wouldn't leave me alone until I agreed to do so. I find it interesting that my classes are filled with as many nonsewers as sewers.

Floorquilting requires no sewing whatsoever and is a very forgiving process. (I may have as many ways to fix mistakes as to create designs!) This book contains all the basic information that you need to make a number of floorquilts, as well as a variety of other projects. It also includes many examples of floorquilts for your idea file.

Floorquilting is like some other crafts—patchwork quilting and floorcloth painting, to name two—but it's also a new craft with some new techniques. Therefore, it's important to read Floorquilt Fundamentals (pages 6–15) carefully before starting on the individual projects. I've included a lot of tips I've picked up in working with floorquilts; maybe you'll discover better, or even easier, ways to do some of the things I discuss. And if you improve on the process, let me know. I continue to learn from my students!

Floorquilt Fundamentals

 TIP Always protect your work surface with a drop cloth.

Personal experience and observation tell me that floorquilting is a nonthreatening, user-friendly technique that will both make you happy and protect your floors. Floorquilts are intended to be functioning floor coverings, so my instructions include a serious number of coatings to give your floorquilts a long life. Water will not damage the finished floorquilt, nor will it be absorbed.

I recommend storing floorquilts flat. You may roll them for shipping, but—especially in cold weather—let them warm to room temperature before unrolling them. The coatings may have hardened because of the cold, and to prevent cracking they'll need time to warm up and soften.

For most of the readers of this book, making floorquilts will be a new and different craft. I present specific instructions for creating a number of floorquilt projects; each project includes the quantity of fabric to treat, number of templates to cut (if required), and size of canvas to prime. A list of required materials used throughout the book follows.

Basic Tools & Materials

The quantities given are enough for a 36″ × 24″ floorquilt.

Essential Materials

- Artist canvas—38″ × 26″ very heavy weight 12-ounce cotton duck primed on one side (**not** floorcloth canvas commercially primed on both sides)

- White acrylic gesso (high quality not required)—8 ounces

- Matte decoupage medium—32 ounces

- Extra-fine 220-grit sandpaper—9″ × 11″ sheet

- Water-based acrylic protective finish (clear satin)—8 ounces

- Clear paste wax (also known as *bowling alley paste wax*)—2 ounces

- Transparent template plastic sheets

- Nonskid rug-backing compound—8 ounces

- Nonskid additive (to add texture to the front of the floorquilt)—1 tablespoon mixed with the final coat of Polycrylic

- 9′ × 12′ plastic drop cloth (2mm)—cut into 3 pieces 9′ × 4′

- White or light cotton fabric (I use muslin) for making pressing cloths, buffing, and lining light fabrics—2 yards

- 3″ sponge brushes—3 per project

- Paintbrush (the stiff, synthetic, inexpensive kind)

- Scissors for cutting paper (don't use your fabric scissors)

- Dark permanent marker

- Yardstick

- Transparent ruler—2″ × 12″ or 2″ × 18″ (I use the gridded C-Thru ruler used for drawing)

- Pencil

- Painter's masking tape

- Steam iron
  (See Sources on page 78 for specific recommendations and where to obtain materials.)

Additional Supplies

- Rotary cutter—with straight and decorative blades

- Pinking shears

- Self-healing cutting mat

- Heavy plastic gridded ruler (often called a *rotary cutting ruler* or *quilt ruler*)—6″ × 24″ is the most versatile size

- Graph paper for creating your own designs—any size grid is fine

- Circle cutter (Fiskars makes a great one; see Sources, page 78) or multicircle templates

- Lightweight fusible interfacing

- Rug padding (a rubbery pad for cushioning)—cut slightly smaller than the floorquilt

- Saral wax-free transfer paper—available in 8¹/₂″ × 11″ sheets or 12″ rolls (amount needed depends on the project)

- Spring-type clothespins (useful as clamps while the floorquilt is drying)

- ¹/₄″ cork sheet for backing trivets (available from art supply, office supply, and craft stores)

- Craft knife

Selecting Fabrics

You will achieve the best results using 100% cotton quilting-weight fabrics, which are generally 44″ wide. The surface should not be highly textured. Home decorating fabrics, such as linen weaves, moirés, failles, damasks, or piles, may produce disappointing results.

Fabrics suitable for floorquilts

TIP

When layering fabrics in floorquilts, darker fabrics (especially prints) may show through lighter fabrics. You can avoid this problem by decoupaging white or off-white fabric to the *wrong* side of the light fabric before cutting out any shapes. Let it dry, and then iron. Treat this fabric as a single layer. I always keep muslin nearby when preparing fabrics for a project; bleached or unbleached muslin works well.

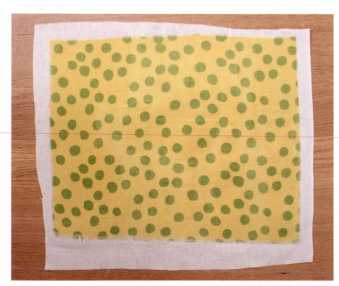

Light fabric backed with muslin

Borders receive the most direct hits from foot traffic wear and tear, but color and design can help disguise this abuse. Medium to dark colors with some design to them work better than lights and solids for borders.

You can choose fabrics to coordinate with the decor of a specific room or select a print, stripe, or plaid "focus fabric" that contains a pleasing combination of colors. This fabric guides the selection of supporting fabrics. It is not necessary to use a large amount of this color-coordinator fabric in the design to have it do the job. In *Turnabout Is Square Play* on page 22, the Westminster print is the focus fabric, doing the job with minimal presence.

Preparing Fabrics

The first step in making any of the floorquilts in this book is to treat the fabric so it will retain the look of fabric while gaining the nonravel, nonstretch, nonbleed, easy-cutting features of paper. Note that these fabrics, like paper, will dull good fabric scissors or rotary cutters. I suggest designating a pair of scissors and a rotary cutter just for cutting treated fabrics.

How-To

1. Spread 2 plastic drop cloths to protect your work area; one under your workspace, and one under your drying fabrics.

2. Mix decoupage medium and water in a 3-to-1 ratio. One cup of the mixture ($^3/4$ cup medium and $^1/4$ cup water) will cover $^3/4$ yard of 44″-wide (27″ × 44″) cotton fabric. If you have leftover medium, you can store the mixture for at least a month in a lidded plastic container.

3. Spread fabrics, right side up, on the drop cloth.

4. Using a sponge brush, apply the diluted decoupage medium to the right side of the fabrics. Clean the sponge brush immediately.

Apply diluted decoupage medium.

5. Move the treated fabrics to another drop cloth, smoothing out any obvious wrinkles, and let dry. If using stripes or plaids, try to keep the lines as straight as possible.

TIP

Plaids and stripes provide nice texture and contrast, but they do present a challenge, especially if being used as long, straight lines. When treating these fabrics, pay extra attention as you lay them flat to dry, carefully smoothing the fabrics and making the lines as straight as possible.

TIP

Don't hang treated fabrics to dry—hanging tends to distort the fabric's design.

6. When the treated fabrics are dry, use a hot iron set on steam, and press them between 2 white or light-colored pressing cloths (to protect both the iron and the ironing surface).

7. The fabrics are now ready to be marked and cut into specific shapes required by your chosen project. Always mark lightly on the back of the fabric and not within the design area. The treatment process may cause heavy marks to appear on the surface of the fabric.

Storing Treated Fabric

Even small leftover bits of treated fabric are worth saving for engineered cutting (also known as *fussy cutting*) or scrappy designs. Think about making a mosaic design or using a narrow strip to decorate a border. Unlike in sewing, in floorquilting you don't need to consider seam allowances or grain.

Folding treated fabric can create permanent creases. Therefore, either store these fabrics flat or rolled onto tubes and secured with masking tape (rubber bands tend to leave crinkles). You can roll and tape small strips without tubes.

Store treated fabrics rolled around a tube.

Preparing Canvas

Very heavy weight 12-ounce acrylic-primed 100% cotton duck canvas is best for making floorquilts (see Sources, page 78). It's heavy enough to last as a floor covering without wearing, curling, or rippling. Before using the canvas in a floorquilt, you must prime it on the raw side (the side that isn't primed) using gesso. Gesso gives the canvas surface a little more texture, less permeability, and added durability.

1. Apply the gesso using a roller, sponge brush, or bristle brush, protecting the work surface with a drop cloth.

Apply gesso to the raw side of the canvas.

2. Place heavy weights along the edges to prevent curling during drying. The primed canvas will shrink slightly after it has dried, so wait until it has dried before trimming off ragged edges and cutting it to the exact size. You can use either side of the canvas as the base for your floorquilt.

TIP

You can use anything heavy—from phone books to canned goods—as a weight. To protect the decoupage, place freezer paper or waxed paper between the weight and the canvas. Either works wonderfully!

Piecing Canvas

Sometimes piecing canvas is necessary for larger floorquilts. It will not be noticeable, because treated fabrics will completely cover the join on the face of the floorquilt.

1. Start with 2 pieces of canvas of the same width. You will need at least an extra 2″ of length on both ends to overlap.
2. Overlap the 2 pieces, and make a light pencil line on both the front and back to help you keep the edges aligned.
3. Working on 1 side at a time, apply full-strength decoupage medium generously between the layers where they overlap. Apply a layer over the join as well. Allow the decoupage to dry thoroughly; then coat the join on the reverse side.
4. After it has dried, reinforce the overlap by using more decoupage medium to apply a 3″-wide strip of muslin (or other light fabric) the entire length of the overlap. Smooth this strip carefully. Dry thoroughly.
5. Trim any excess canvas or muslin. The side with the muslin will be the back of the floorquilt.

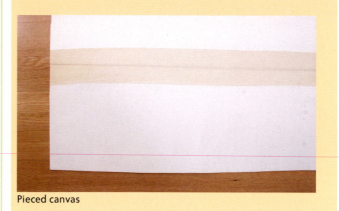

Pieced canvas

Central Design

The term *central design* simply refers to everything within a floorquilt's borders. The central design makes up the majority of the floorquilt's real estate and makes the floorquilt distinct.

The central design of each floorquilt in this book is different, so the processes needed to create these areas are different as well. I've included specific instructions within each of the projects. **Always apply the central design area before adding borders.**

TIP

The fear of miscutting a special fabric can lead you to use a safer, less interesting choice for a project. My solution? Make color photocopies of these special fabrics (or scan and print them) to test them in design placement. Cut pieces from the paper copies until you find the cut you like. Use leftover photocopies as gift wrap!

Applying Borders

After you have completed the central designs, follow these steps to apply the borders to all the floorquilts and smaller projects in this book. (If it is necessary to "piece" fabric strips to create the border, it is best done on the two opposing sides that are applied first. Try to make the join in an inconspicuous area of the fabric's design, and allow at least a 1″ overlap.)

TIP

Stripes placed perpendicular to the edge make effective borders—and wiggles and joins tend not to show because the lines are relatively short. Bias-cut plaids and stripes also tend to hide wiggles, and bias always adds interest to a design.

Photo by Tom Young

How-To

1. Using a ruler and rotary cutter or scissors, cut the 4 border strips according to the dimensions given for the specific floorquilt. The border strips for the 2 longer sides will be the same length as the longer measurement of the canvas. The strips for the 2 shorter sides will always be at least 2″ longer than the sides themselves. All outer border strips are cut at least 1″ wider than needed; the extra width will be folded over to the back.

TIP

I find that using a rotary cutter, heavy plastic ruler, and self-healing mat to cut border strips is a huge help—the cutting goes faster and is generally much more accurate. Just be sure you cut 1 layer at a time, and do not fold the fabric.

Cut border strips carefully.

2. Using full-strength decoupage medium and a sponge brush, apply the medium to the wrong sides of the top and bottom border strips to adhere them in place. Always apply the borders that are cut the same length as the floorquilt first, allowing an extra 1″ along the long edges to be folded over to the back. Let dry.

Decoupage the first border strips into place.

3. Turn the long edges to the back of the canvas, finger-pressing the fold, and decoupage them into place. It may be necessary to apply weights to the folded edges of the borders (or use spring-type clothespins) to create a secure bond. Let dry.

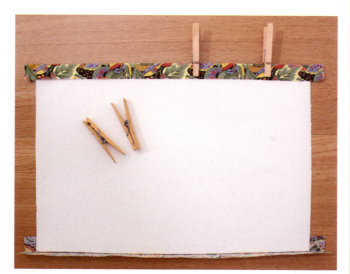

Fold borders to the back, decoupage, and secure with clothespins.

4. After the folded strips have dried, trim off any excess fabric on the ends, if necessary, making them even with the edges of the canvas.

Trim fabric even with canvas.

5. On the front, decoupage the 2 shorter border strips into place with 1″ extra at each end and along the long edges, covering any uneven edges on the central design. If necessary, you can use weights or spring-type clothespins to ensure a secure bond. Let dry.

Apply the 2 short strips and let dry.

6. Trim the ends 1″ beyond the ends of the canvas, and fold the 1″ flaps of the short sides to the back of the canvas. Decoupage them into place, using weights or spring-type clothespins if necessary. Let dry.

Fold and decoupage the 1″ flaps to the back.

7. Turn the remaining short sides over the edges to the back of the canvas, finger-pressing the fold. Decoupage the folded fabric to the back of the canvas, using weights or spring-type clothespins if necessary. Let dry thoroughly.

Border Variations

Double Borders

Multiple borders are a nice option to consider when designing a floorquilt. In *Turnabout Is Square Play* (page 22), I cut the narrow inner border from the floorquilt's focus fabric so that it acts to unify all the colors in the design.

After I prepared and cut the canvas, I penciled a line 3˝ in from all 4 edges to define the border and central design areas. After finishing the central design, I cut and applied the narrow border strips, using them to even out any minor flaws in the edges of the central design. The corners can be overlapped, or they can be cut to appear mitered by cutting the top strip's overlap at a 45° angle.

I applied the second and wider borders as indicated in Applying Borders (page 11). I used the same technique in creating the bright inner border in *Butterflies & Vines* (page 43).

In the *Mitered Squares* floorquilt (page 20) and *Folk Flowers* (page 27), I applied the smaller borders directly onto finished borders. Their placement allows a slight amount of the primary border to appear between the applied border and the central design area, giving the appearance of a triple border.

TIP

When designing your floorquilts, be sure to allow at least an extra 1˝ for the border strips to be turned to the back. Allow less than 1˝ and it won't stay put!

Pieced Border Designs

The outermost border receives the most wear, and it should not be heavily pieced for this reason. If you want the look of a pieced border, create a pieced inner border —which certainly can be wider than the real outer border—or apply a pieced strip onto a wide border.

I pieced the narrow border applied to the wider border in *Folk Flowers,* shown in the photo below, using scraps from the prepared fabrics left over from the central design. I used the fusible interfacing technique described on page 35 in *Horizontal Strips/Vertical Bars*.

I recommend using this fusible interfacing technique for any pieced borders. Just keep the pieced borders away from the outermost edges of the floorquilt, as these areas receive the most wear. Multiple edges would be damaged more easily than would a continuous piece of prepared fabric.

Narrow applied border

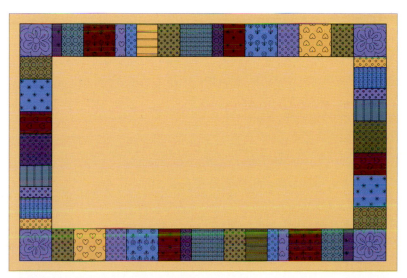

Wide pieced border and solid outer border

Applying Protective Coatings & Backing

To ensure the durability of your floorquilts, apply several layers of protective coatings to each one: decoupage medium, water-based acrylic finish, and a final coat of paste wax. In addition, add nonskid materials to both the surface and backing to make them safe and nonslippery. See Sources on page 78 if you have trouble finding any of these materials.

Decoupage Medium

1. Place the floorquilt face up on a clean drop cloth.

2. With the sponge brush used for treating the fabrics, apply an even coat of full-strength decoupage medium to the entire face of the floorquilt.

Apply full-strength decoupage medium.

3. Carefully press out any bubbles or wrinkles in the floorquilt, and press down edges or corners that are not secure. Run your hand over the front and back perimeters of the floorquilt to wipe away any residual decoupage medium. Let the floorquilt dry. (Drying may take anywhere from an hour to 4 hours, depending on the humidity.)

4. Repeat this coating process twice, for a total of 3 coats of full-strength decoupage medium. Dry for 24 hours.

Acrylic Finishing Coat

1. Stir, do not shake, the can of water-based acrylic finish before using.

2. With a new sponge brush (brushing in one direction and not overbrushing), apply a coat of acrylic finish.

Apply acrylic finish.

3. Allow at least 2 hours to dry. Then lightly sand the surface with fine sandpaper (220 grit), removing any dust with a damp cloth when you have finished sanding.

Sand the surface lightly between coats of acrylic.

4. Repeat Steps 1 through 3 to add a second coat of acrylic finish.

5. Repeat Steps 1 through 3 again, but this time add a nonskid additive such as Skid-Tex (see Sources, page 78) to the final coat of acrylic finish. Follow the manufacturer's instructions for quantity and setup time. After the third coat, allow the floorquilt to dry completely (24 hours or more if necessary). **Note: The nonskid additive is not needed for off-the-floor projects.**

TIP

Include a nonskid additive when applying the final coat of acrylic finish to prevent slipping.

Paste Wax

1. Using a slightly moistened soft cloth, apply a thin coat of clear paste wax over the top of the entire floorquilt.

2. When the wax has dried, buff gently (not to a high shine) with a clean, soft cloth. Do not walk on the floorquilt for 24 hours. **Note: The paste wax is not needed for off-the-floor projects.**

Apply clear paste wax to the face of the finished floorquilt.

TIP

In high-traffic areas, remove the paste wax about every 6 months with any household cleaner (for example, Fantastik, Formula 409, or Simple Green), and reapply.

Nonskid Backing

Using a synthetic-bristle paintbrush, apply a thin, even coat of nonskid backing such as Saf-T-Bak (see Sources on page 78) to the back of the floorquilt. Doing so will prevent the floorquilt from slipping—without damaging floors. Allow the backing to dry at least 24 hours before use. The nonskid backing will appear white when dry. **Note: The nonskid backing is not needed for off-the-floor projects.**

Time to Make a Floorquilt

I've included a variety of floorquilt styles and designs in the following chapters and given complete instructions for a basic style. For example, the next chapter, Squares Dancing, features designs composed of squares. I've provided complete and detailed instructions for Handkerchief Corners (page 17). Following the basic project are photos and descriptions of similar floorquilts that you can create using the same techniques. The geometric designs allow you to easily create floorquilts to fit your specific size requirements by simply increasing the number or size of the blocks, borders, or both.

Try your hand at floorquilting by making one of the basic projects. The soaring confidence you will develop after completing one floorquilt is all you need to tackle future projects. You can easily create a customized version of one of the *projects* or *inspirations* featured in this book.

Portion of a floorquilt by Degan Sayer, photo by Parsley Steinweiss

Squares Dancing

The designs of many quilts, old and new, are composed of squares. Using squares allows for an endless variety of designs. Following is a tiny portion of the possibilities that you can achieve using the humble square. With floorquilting, you can make pleasing and amazing geometric designs from your scrap bag or fabrics purchased specifically for the project. The process is fun and easy, giving fabrics the no-sew characteristics of paper.

Handkerchief Corners

This "training wheels" floorquilt will reward your efforts and provide you with a new skill to enjoy and be proud of. But beware: making floorquilts is so easy that making one is never enough! Select fabrics containing a pleasing combination of colors. In this case, the colors of the focus fabric used as the border are more important than the actual design, because they will guide all of your other selections. Your focus fabric can be one of the fat quarters, or it can be the border if the design lends itself to acting as a frame.

Pretty in Pink
Finished block: 6″ × 6″
Finished floorquilt: 36″ × 24″

Photo by Tom Young

Materials

- Basic tools and materials (page 7)
- Treated canvas (page 10) cut to 36″ × 24″
- Transparent template plastic, 1 sheet (12″ × 18″)
- Treated fabrics (page 8):

  8 to 10 fat quarters (18″ × 22″)

  ½ yard medium to dark (preferably not a solid) for border

Construction

1. Pencil a centered 18″ × 30″ rectangle on one side of the treated canvas, creating 3″-wide borders on all sides.

2. Use scissors or a rotary cutter and ruler to cut 4 squares—6″, 5″, 4″, and 3″—from the template plastic.

TIP

Using graph paper to draw the squares ensures true right angles.

3. Identify each template by size with a permanent marker. (These templates will come in handy for many other projects.)

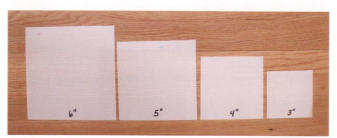

Plastic templates

4. Trace 2 or 3 squares of each size on the backs of the treated fat quarters. Cut out the squares.

5. Mark and cut 4 border strips—2 strips 4″ × 36″ and 2 strips 4″ × 26″—from the treated border fabric.

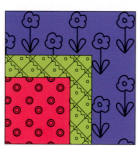

Sample Handkerchief Corners block

6. Following the illustration and photo below, arrange the squares in layers to create at least 20 blocks 6″ × 6″. A block may contain many different-sized squares or only 1 or 2. Refer to the photograph on page 74 to see the variety in *Kornering Kaffe Fassett & Friends*.

Arrange squares in layers.

7. Using decoupage medium full strength, decoupage the layered squares into place to create the 6″ blocks, being careful to press out any noticeable bubbles or wrinkles. Let the blocks dry. You need 15 blocks for this floorquilt, so there will be plenty of blocks to choose from. See Off-the-Floorquilts beginning on page 61 for suggestions on using leftover blocks.

TIP

Wash your hands frequently during this process, as the decoupage medium builds up on the hands and flakes off onto the work in progress. I keep a bucket of soapy water and an old towel nearby.

To keep gluey flakes away from fabric and fingers, use a piece of clean, transparent plastic when smoothing out bubbles or pressing down edges.

TIP

If you want to make a Handkerchief Corners floorquilt that uses multiples of the same block design, make concentric square blocks twice the required size, and cut them into 4 equal parts.

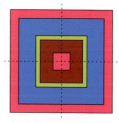

For example, make 12 ″ blocks (instead of 6 ″ blocks), and cut them into quarters. A rotary cutter and ruler make this easier.

If it's necessary to move the project before decoupaging the blocks into place, make a simple block placement diagram. Mark the corresponding placement numbers on pieces of masking tape on the fronts of the blocks.

1A	1B	1C	1D	1E
2A	2B	2C	2D	2E
3A	3B	3C	3D	3E

Block placement diagram

8. Using full-strength decoupage medium, decoupage the blocks into place on the canvas within the 18″ × 30″ rectangle. Again, wash hands frequently to avoid transferring flakes of dried medium to the floorquilt. Let everything dry thoroughly.

9. Follow the instructions for Applying Borders (page 11).

10. Follow the instructions in Applying Protective Coatings & Backing (page 14).

11. Everything dry? Congratulations! You've finished your first floorquilt!

Other Options

As you constructed this traditional design, it may have become obvious that you can create many more designs using squares. With the ease of decoupage, anything is possible. There are no floorquilt rules that forbid combining multiple block designs in a single project. The floor's the limit!

These floorquilts—from my first-time students at the Quilt Cottage in Mamaroneck, New York—offer plenty of inspiration. The students delighted in learning the basics and promptly did their own things. I proudly share their results. You can see some of the floorquilts in greater detail in the Gallery (pages 71–76).

Floorquilts made by students.

Photo by Parsley Steinweiss

Mitered Squares

Mitered designs look a lot more complicated than they really are, which makes producing one of these floorquilts especially satisfying. Try selecting an irregularly striped fabric—it provides more interesting and unexpected possibilities for the corners.

Mitered Lemon Squares
Finished block: 5″ × 5″
Finished floorquilt: 34″ × 24″

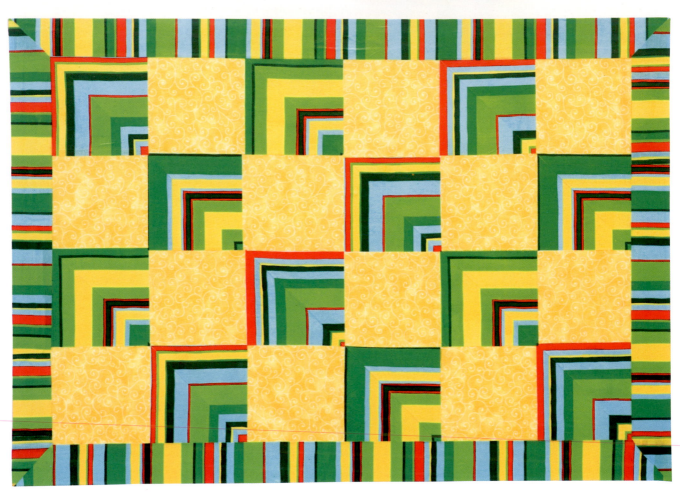

Materials

- Basic tools and materials (page 7)
- Treated canvas (page 10) cut to 34″ × 24″
- Transparent template plastic—1 square, 5″ × 5″
- Treated fabrics (page 8):
  ¹/₂ yard solid
  1¹/₄ yards stripe

Construction

1. From the striped fabric, cut 2 crosswise border strips 3″ × 34″ and 2 strips 3″ × 26″. The stripes should run perpendicular to the long edges.

2. From the solid fabric, cut 12 squares 5″ × 5″ each. Draw around the transparent plastic template for accuracy on the wrong side of the fabric.

3. Select 2 interesting 5″-wide areas of the striped fabric, and cut a 32″-long strip of each.

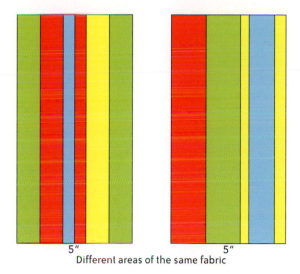

5"   5"
Different areas of the same fabric

4. Cut 6 squares 5″ × 5″ from each lengthwise striped section for a total of 12 squares.

5. Working with pairs, draw a diagonal line on each square, as shown below. Label the triangles A through H, writing the letters on small pieces of masking tape and placing them on the appropriate sections. Cut each square on the dotted diagonal line to produce 3 triangles of each letter.

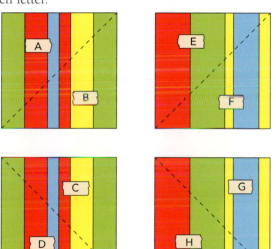

Label and cut squares.

6. Arrange the triangles as shown, making 3 each of the 4 different mitered squares.

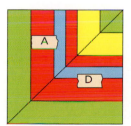 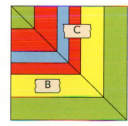 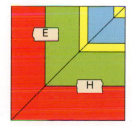 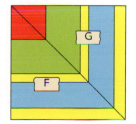

Make 3 of each.

7. Temporarily hold the squares together with masking tape.

8. Pencil a centered 30″ × 20″ rectangle on one side of the canvas, creating a 2″ border on all sides.

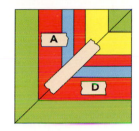

9. Lay out the taped-together mitered squares, alternating them with solid squares, within the penciled borders. Play with their placement until the design pleases you; then remove the masking tape.

10. Decoupage all the solid and mitered squares into place with full-strength medium. They should fit perfectly within the 30″ × 20″ rectangle you have drawn. Let the squares dry.

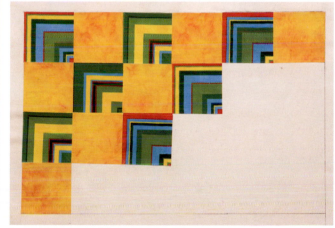

Arrange squares and decoupage into place.

11. Follow the instructions in Applying Borders (page 11) but cut the short borders at a 45° angle. Decoupage them into place on top of the long borders instead of completely overlapping them. This will create the look of a miter.

12. Let the borders dry thoroughly. Then follow the instructions in Applying Protective Coatings & Backing (page 14).

13. Ta da! Another floorquilt completed! See more examples of Mitered Squares in the Gallery (pages 71–76).

Turnabout Is Square Play

I made the 6″-square blocks for this floorquilt using various sizes of square transparent plastic templates, as described on page 18 for the Handkerchief Corners design. The assembly process for making the blocks and adding the borders is the same as well.

The color combination was inspired by the delightful Kaffe Fassett printed stripe of reds, pinks, oranges, and greens shown below. I added narrow strips of this fabric as an inner border that defines the central design.

Finished block: 6″ × 6″
Finished floorquilt: 28″ × 22″

Printed stripe fabric by Kaffe Fassett for Westminster Fabrics

Circles Within Squares

Circles and squares are pleasing shapes; when used together in a positive/negative grid, they produce a nicely balanced design. Notice that the addition of red squares applied onto the lighter shade of its border brings the border of this floorquilt to life.

Finished block: 6″ × 6″
Finished floorquilt: 30″ × 24″

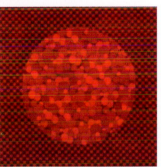

This floorquilt features a turquoise and red print in the border that is echoed in the central design.

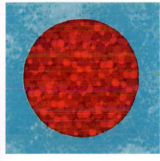

Four-Patch With Scalloped Leaves

This floorquilt's structure, a four-patch block alternating with a solid block, is easily recognized as a traditional quilt design. I chose to add the scalloped leaf "appliqué" to the solid square for fun, but this basic pattern can emerge from your imagination in countless ways.

Finished leaf block: 4″ × 4″
Finished four-patch block: 4″ × 4″
Finished floorquilt: 40″ × 28″

Materials

- Basic tools and materials (page 7)
- Treated canvas (page 10) cut to 40″ × 28″
- Treated fabrics (page 8):
  - 1/2 yard gold
  - 1/3 yard red
  - 1/4 yard green
  - 3/8 yard black geometric
  - 3/8 yard rust batik
  - 1/2 yard complementary border fabric*
- Transparent template plastic, 10″ × 6″
- Rotary cutter with a scalloped blade, or pinking shears
- Masking tape

If your border fabric is less than 42″ wide, you will need to piece the border or buy 1¼ yards of fabric and cut the borders on the lengthwise grain.

Construction

1. Cut treated fabrics as follows:
   - 2″ black geometric squares—cut 54.
   - 2″ rust batik squares—cut 54.
   - 4″ gold squares—cut 27.
   - 3″ × 30″ strips of border fabric—cut 2.
   - 3″ × 40″ strips of border fabric—cut 2.

2. Trace the pattern for the leaf and stem on page 26 onto a 4″ square of template plastic using a dark permanent marker.

3. Make individual templates for the leaf and stem by tracing each outline onto the remaining piece of plastic. Cut out both pieces. Indicate fronts and backs with the permanent marker.

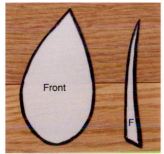

Front of templates

4. With a pencil, trace 27 leaves onto the back of the leaf (red) fabric. (Remember that the shapes will be reversed when turned over.) Use either side of the templates; just be consistent for both leaf and stem.

5. Cut out the leaves with pinking shears or a rotary cutter with a scalloped blade.

6. Follow the same procedure for the stems (green), but use a regular blade.

7. Using masking tape along the top edge, attach the square leaf and stem template to your work surface prepared for decoupage. The tape will act as a hinge.

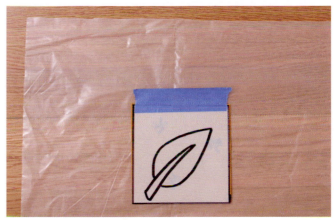

Tape template to work surface.

8. Position a leaf under the template. Apply a thin coat of decoupage medium to the back of a stem. Doing so puts the medium only where it is needed. Raise the template, and position the stem onto the leaf according to the outline. Repeat with all stems and leaves.

9. Position a gold 4″ square exactly under the template.

10. Apply a thin coat of decoupage medium to the back of a leaf unit, raise the template, and position each leaf unit onto the gold square, following the outline. Press out any wrinkles or bubbles.

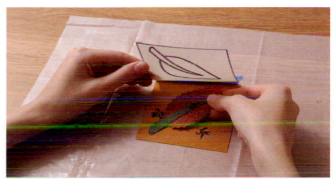

Place leaf unit onto gold square under template.

11. Mark a centered rectangle 36″ × 24″ on the canvas for the central design, creating a 2″ border all around.

12. Arrange the 2″ squares into Four-Patch blocks and alternate them with the leaf blocks on the canvas, according to the photo. Decoupage the squares, and allow them to dry.

13. Using the 3″ strips of border fabric, follow the instructions in Applying Borders (page 11). Let dry.

14. Follow the instructions in Applying Protective Coatings & Backing (page 14).

Leaf and Stem Pattern

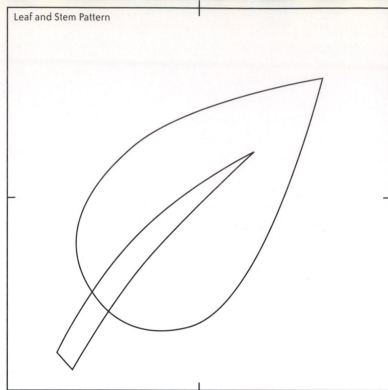

Folk Flower Pattern

Folk Flowers

This project only looks difficult. The Handkerchief Corners blocks are made up of different-sized squares, stacked in descending order, aligned at a corner. There is a color scheme of predominantly red, yellow, and green, but the fabrics are scrappy. These same scraps make up the $^1/_2$" inner border, applied to the 4"-wide red border. A pattern for the flower block is provided on page 26.

Finished block: 6˝ × 6˝
Finished floorquilt: 44˝ × 32˝

1. Follow the instructions for making the Handkerchief Corners blocks (page 17).

2. Make flower and leaf templates out of transparent template plastic by tracing and cutting out the patterns provided on page 26.

3. Cut shapes from treated fabrics, using a decorative rotary blade or pinking shears to add interest to leaves and stems if desired.

4. Make the flower blocks following the instructions for the leaf blocks in *Four-Patch With Scalloped Leaves* on page 25.

Scrap Happy

The floorquilts in this chapter are categorized as scrappy for obvious reasons: they appear to have been pulled together out of the scrap basket! True or not, the casual mood achieved by successfully mixing so many fabrics has a pleasing softness.

Penny Rug

I painted the canvas background on this floorquilt black. The "pennies" created from a variety of fabulous fabrics really pop. Have fun combining circles of brightly colored fabrics. Note that I simplified the instructions so that the floorquilt will have only one narrow border.

Pennies From the Scrap Basket
Finished floorquilt: 36″ × 24″

Materials

- Basic tools and materials (page 7)
- Treated canvas (page 10) cut to 36″ × 24″
- Flat black latex paint, 8 ounces
- Paintbrush
- Circle cutter or 1 sheet (8$^{1}/_{2}$″ × 11″) of transparent template plastic (see Sources, page 78)
- Treated fabrics (page 8):
  $^{1}/_{3}$ yard each of at least 10 complementary fabrics— a mix of light, medium, and dark values
  $^{1}/_{3}$ yard of border fabric

- 24″ transparent ruler
- 8″ × 10″ cardstock or 2 index cards

Construction

1. Paint a side of the treated canvas with black latex paint, and allow to dry thoroughly.

2. Cut 2 strips 2″ × 36″ and 2 strips 2″ × 26″ from treated border fabric.

3. If using template plastic, make circle templates 2″, 2¹/₂″, 3″, 3¹/₂″, and 4″ in diameter. Cut circles with a circle cutter or by tracing around the circle templates onto the *wrong* side of the fabrics and hand cutting. Cut at least 40 circles 4″ in diameter and at least 35 circles of *each* of the other diameters from the treated fabrics.

TIP

A circle cutter will cut all the sizes needed quickly and easily. They are available at craft stores, or see Sources (page 78). Alternatively, you can use a compass to draw circles of several sizes on paper; then trace the circles onto template plastic and cut out to make the templates.

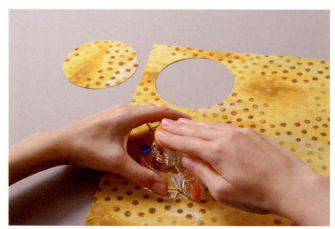

Circle cutter at work

4. Play with all the various circles until you have at least 40 concentric designs that please you and work well together. Be sure to use a 4″ circle on the bottom of each stack. Use anywhere from 2 to 5 circles in each stack.

5. Decoupage the circle sets together. Allow them to dry.

6. On the painted canvas, apply 1″ painter's tape or masking tape around the entire edge.

7. Cut 2 strips from the cardstock or index cards: ¹/₂″ × 4″ and ¹/₄″ × 4″.

8. Referring to the floorquilt assembly diagram on page 31, place the left row of 5 circles (A1–E1) next to the masking tape, using the ¹/₂″ card strip for even placement. Decoupage these circle sets into place.

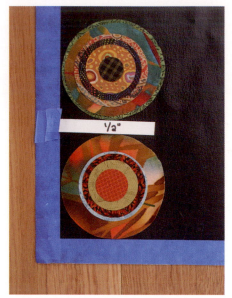

Decoupage left row of circles in place.

9. Place the bottom row of 8 circle sets (E2–E8) next to the masking tape, using the ¹/₄″ card strip for even placement. Decoupage into place.

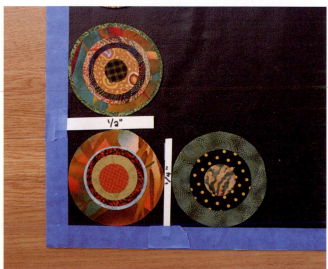

Arrange and decoupage the bottom row.

10. Position a 24″ transparent ruler vertically and aligned with the right edge of circle E2; mark the top strip of masking tape. This will be the placement guide for the right side of circle set A2. Using this method, mark the upper tape for placement of the remaining A circles. A8 fits into the upper right corner created by the top and right-side masking tape strips.

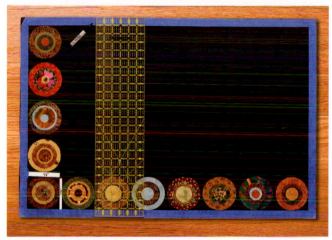

Mark placement for the next vertical row.

11. Using the 24″ ruler and the ½″ and ¼″ card strips as guides, lay out the rest of the circle sets in horizontal rows.

Arrange circles in horizontal rows.

12. Make any necessary adjustments, and decoupage into place. Let dry.

13. Remove masking tape, and mark a ¾″ border on all sides.

14. Follow the instructions in Applying Borders (page 11). You will fold 1¼″ of the border strips to the back. Refer to Applying Protective Coatings & Backing (page 14) to finish your floorquilt.

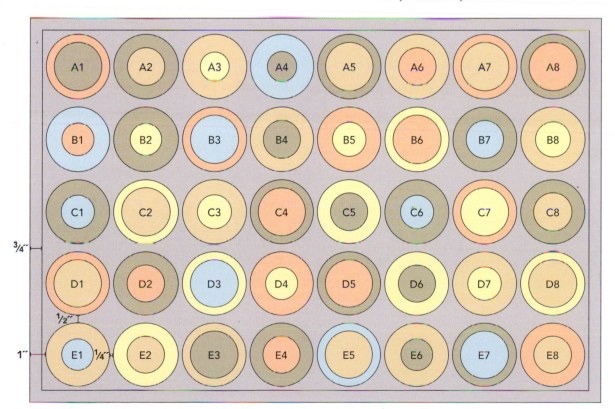

Floorquilt Assembly Diagram

Hanging Diamonds

This floorquilt could easily be created using squares on point, but I chose to illustrate a slightly different shape called a hanging diamond. *To make templates for this shape, trace the diamond patterns from page 33, and label each size.*

Diamonds Underfoot
Finished floorquilt: 43˝ × 35˝

Diamond Patterns

Notice in the floorquilt photo that there are no rules as to how many concentric diamonds make a good design. I used a decorative rotary blade to cut out all the inner diamonds in order to provide a little more texture to the design. The outermost diamonds must all be cut straight in order to fit next to one another with no gaps.

If you would like to have a dominant color in your scrappy floorquilt, alternate scrappy diamonds with solid diamonds of that color. This technique will make each scrappy diamond stand on its own as a design, and half of the floorquilt will be in your featured color. In *Diamonds Underfoot,* I took a more subtle approach by using a blue fabric for all the outermost half-diamonds and ending with a narrow border.

Horizontal Strips/ Vertical Bars

The common thread running among the fabrics in this earth-toned floorquilt is the hand-dyed aspect of the fabrics. This design will easily lend itself to any size, proportion, or color combination you can think of. As an added bonus, it's a breeze to make, thanks to lightweight fusible interfacing—a thin, nonwoven sheet that has heat-activated adhesive on one side (see Sources, page 78).

Finished floorquilt: 43 ″ × 32 ″

1. Cut rectangles of varying widths from treated fabrics. After you have cut more rectangles than you could possibly need, lay them in rows on a surface next to the ironing board.

Arrange rectangles in rows.

2. All of these small pieces will be held together in order by ironing them onto a strip of lightweight fusible interfacing $1/2''$ narrower than the fabric rectangles and as long as the project requires (so the adhesive does not stick to the hot iron).

3. Place the fusible interfacing adhesive side up on an ironing board. Position the rectangles in order onto the adhesive side of the fusible interfacing, and iron. This step makes their placement onto the treated canvas very easy. Instead of decoupaging each individual piece into place, you are now working with one big strip—speeding up the process immeasurably.

Iron fabric strips onto fusible interfacing.

4. Trim the fused strip to the desired width.

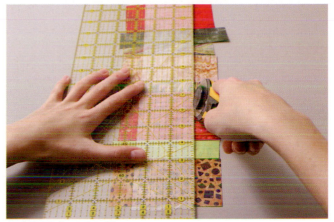

Cut strip to desired width.

5. Use the fused strip in your floorquilt design.

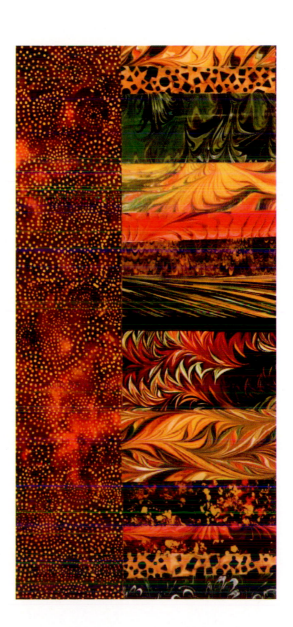

For the Love of Fabric

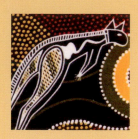

The floorquilt designs in this chapter were created specifically to showcase beautiful fabrics, supporting the beauty created by the textile artists. First, however, I had to confront and overcome my "I don't want to cut that fabulous fabric!" issues.

Marbled Diamonds

These glorious fabrics, hand marbled by Marjorie Lee Bevis, are so spectacular that adding anything else would create an unfortunate distraction. The simple graphics of this linear design of adjoining diamonds contrast with and enhance the liquidity of the marbling.

Finished floorquilt: 38″ × 26″

Finished floorquilt: 35½″ × 32″

Bush Banana

*The featured fabric is called **Bush Banana** by Donna Abbots, its Aboriginal designer. I was thrilled when it arrived from Australia, and I knew it was ready to become a floorquilt. I stared at it on the design wall—up, down, and sideways—studying the vibrant elements of its design. There were many things I could do with the individual elements, but nothing compared with what Donna Abbots had already done.*

I focused on that wonderful explosion of colors representing a bush banana flower and worked my way outward. I included several auxiliary motifs, creating a generous, slightly off-center design. When I found the four kangaroos in a basket of special scraps, the rest of the design took shape.

The bush banana and the four cornered kangaroos needed framing. The measurements of these five elements dictated the size of the finished floorquilt. I selected the supporting fabrics to complement, but not compete with, the star of the show. Creating this piece was an indulgence that still makes me smile.

Be a Cutup

The following designs are examples of what quilters call engineered design or fussy cutting—the practice of selecting desired elements of a fabric's design as you cut. I fussy cut motifs to be reborn as insects, butterfly wings, or caterpillar sections. The butterflies and caterpillars in Butterflies & Vines (page 43) hail from non-zoological origins, and the medieval floral sprigs in Flowering Irish Chain (page 42) began life as paisley parts, batiks, or unrecognizable flora. Those of us insane enough to enjoy this sort of treasure hunt for designs within designs find it as much fun as two desserts!

Trellis & Toile

This floorquilt can be easily designed around any repeated motif in a fabric. I used scenes in a toile fabric that fit nicely into a 14″ square. Smaller scenes can be framed by (or mounted onto) a larger piece to create a 14″ square.

Finished floorquilt: 108″ × 87″

Materials

- Basic tools and materials (page 7)
- Circle cutter or 4″-diameter template
- Treated canvas (page 10) cut to 108″ × 87″
- Treated fabrics (page 8):
  3¼ to 4 yards of toile or other focus fabric*
  2 yards plaid for sashing
  3¼ yards dark fabric for triangles and outer border†
  ⅜ yard fabric for 5″ squares at sashing intersections
  2 yards fabric for inner border†
- Rulers—6″-wide transparent ruler and 1 ruler at least 36″ long

Yardage of focus fabric needed may vary depending on the spacing and repeat pattern. Refer to Construction (page 40) for cutting dimensions and quantity.

†*Yardage allows for borders to be cut crosswise and pieced from 42″-wide fabric.*

TIP

After selecting the design motif and other fabrics, pay close attention to measuring and marking the canvas. This process is somewhat tedious, but the result is worth it.

Construction

1. From the toile fabric:

   Cut 13 squares 14″ × 14″.

   Cut 4 rectangles 14″ × 3½″.

   Cut 12 circles 4″ in diameter.

2. From the plaid fabric cut 24 sashing strips 5″ × 19¾″.

3. From the dark fabric:

   Cut 25 squares 10″ × 10″; cut them in half diagonally once to create 50 triangles.

   Cut 4 squares 3½″ × 3½″; cut them in half diagonally once to create 8 triangles.

   Cut 11 strips 2″ wide, to make 2 outer border strips that will finish at 1″ × 108″ and 2 outer border strips that will finish at 1″ × 89″. See page 10 for piecing instructions.

4. From the inner border fabric cut 11 strips 4″ wide, to make 2 borders 4″ × 98″ and 2 borders 4″ × 85″. See page 10 for piecing instructions.

5. From the fabric for squares at sashing intersections, cut 12 squares 5″ × 5″.

6. Following the illustration on page 41, carefully draw the lines onto the canvas. First lightly pencil the 1″ and 4″ borders onto the canvas. Then check to make sure your center design area is 98″ × 77″. Make adjustments in the border as needed, and make certain that the drawn corners are exact right angles (90°). Completing ¼ of the design will make the remaining ¾ easier.

TIP

Long straight-edge devices are helpful (as long as they are truly straight) for connecting all the points in a straight line.

7. Place the 14″ toile squares in position, and trim them to fit as needed along the edges. Decoupage the toile squares in place. Then, following the photo, decoupage the 14″ × 3½″ toile rectangles in place, trimming them if needed. This is a large project, and no matter how carefully you measure and draw, some spaces may be slightly off.

Toile placement

TIP

If you find that one of your treated fabric pieces is slightly too small for the drawn space, cut a filler piece from scraps, and decoupage it into place. It will blend in and be undetectable in the finished floorquilt.

8. Decoupage the triangles in place.

9. Decoupage the sashing strips and then the small 5″ squares at the sashing intersections.

10. Apply the 4″ circles of motif fabric onto the 5″ squares.

11. Decoupage the longer pieced 4″ borders to the top and bottom of the floorquilt, then add the shorter 4″ borders.

12. To add the 1″ outer border, use the 2″ strips of dark fabric and follow the instructions in Applying Borders (page 11).

13. Follow the instructions in Applying Protective Coatings & Backing (page 14).

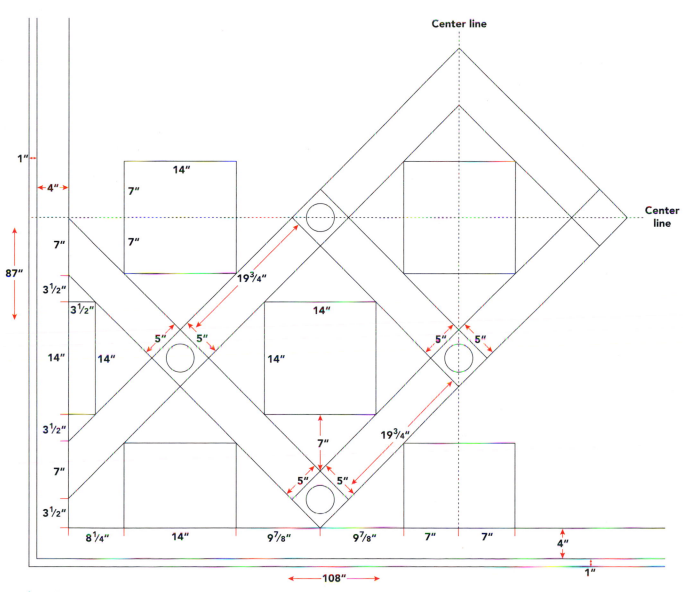

Center line

Center line

1"

4"

14"

7"

7"

7"

87"

19³/₄"

3¹/₂"

3¹/₂"

14"

14"

14"

14"

14"

5"

5"

5"

5"

7"

3¹/₂"

19³/₄"

7"

5"

5"

3¹/₂"

8¹/₄"

14"

9⁷/₈"

9⁷/₈"

7"

7"

4"

1"

108"

¹/₄ of Floorquilt Layout

Flowering Irish Chain

This floorquilt, which measures almost 9´ × 6´, is the first one I ever made—clear evidence that this craft is enjoyable from day one.

The diagonal grid is made of three rows of side-by-side squares (a variation of the traditional Irish Chain quilt block). By choosing to create a different fantasy floral sprig in each diamond, I eliminated the fear of not having enough fabric. I had total freedom to plow through my scrap basket looking for motifs that could become a bloom or a bug, and that would show up on a red background.

Although the design could be interpreted in fabric as a hand-appliquéd quilt, it would require a certain amount of skill and many hours to achieve. As a floorquilt, it is successfully executed in a fraction of the time with scissors, a sense of adventure, and the willingness to see a fabric's design motifs as something beyond their original purpose.

Finished floorquilt: 105˝ × 71˝

Floral sprigs and insects in this floorquilt began life as something entirely different

Photo by Tom Young

Butterflies & Vines

This deceptively simple floorquilt is composed of individual blocks set on point, which were completed individually and then assembled on the canvas. This floorquilt gives you yet another opportunity to let your imagination loose while you engineer fabrics into butterflies, blossoms, and caterpillars.

Finished floorquilt: 63˝ × 55˝

TIP

Just as flowers and bugs were prime subjects for fussy cutting in *Flowering Irish Chain* (page 42), butterflies also lend themselves to fussy cutting.

Butterflies come in so many shapes that our minds easily accept variations to accommodate a fabric's particularly interesting motif. They are equally fun to visualize when you look at fabric prints of fish, flowers, paisley, or batik; it becomes easy to see areas custom-made to be fussy cut into graceful wings of butterflies and moths. Crawling caterpillars simply composed of overlapping circles cut from a dense, repeated design easily inhabit the floorquilt's design edge.

To illustrate the numerous possibilities in fussy cutting small-repeat designs, note that all twelve of the small yellow flowers at the vine intersections are different, yet were cut from just two fabrics.

Because of the labor-intensive nature of the projects I lay out for myself, when I create fussy-cut appliqué quilts, even friends whisper "psychological abnormality" behind my back. When they learn how painlessly simple it is to make the same design as a floorquilt, they are willing to reevaluate my mental status!

TIP

The yellow flowers were applied after all of the blocks were decoupaged into place, to add spots of color and hide any possible gaps where the 4 blocks meet. This technique is also useful for protecting areas where many points come together.

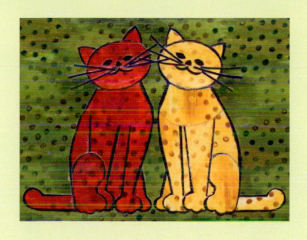

Whimsy Underfoot

The following floorquilts can be described as "task oriented." The pet dining mats serve double duty—not only protecting floors from messy four-footed eaters but also showing those sloppy slurpers that they are special enough to have custom "table" coverings.

Boo!

Finished floorquilt: 39ʺ × 28ʺ

Materials

- Basic tools and materials (page 7)
- Wax-free transfer paper—2 sheets 8½ʺ × 11ʺ, or 16ʺ from a 12ʺ-wide roll
- Lightweight poster board or heavy paper such as oak tag—2 sheets 17ʺ × 22ʺ
- Treated canvas (page 10) cut to 39ʺ × 28ʺ
- Treated fabrics (page 8):
  - ¾ yard lime green (background)
  - ⅝ yard black (spiderweb and cat)
  - ⅝ yard black with orange dot (Boo)
  - ¼ yard (or fat eighth) purple (spider)
  - ½ yard black tone-on-tone (bats)
  - ⅝ yard orange with black dot (border)
- Gluestick
- Hole punch

Construction

1. Enlarge the central design on page 48 by 400%. Some piecing of the copies will be required. Trace the patterns for the bat and spider; enlarge and trace the cat pattern (pages 49 and 50).

TIP

Use the original copy for making notes and labeling parts of the spiderweb.

2. Transfer all the design elements from Step 1 onto poster board or oak tag using wax-free transfer paper.

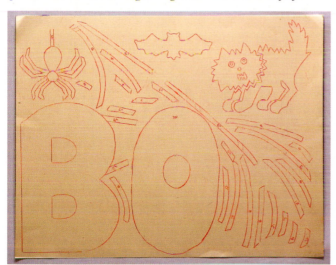

Transfer pattern pieces to poster board.

3. Cut out each poster board pattern. Mark and label the front and back of each piece. The spiderweb segments should be about $1/2$″ wide.

4. Draw a centered rectangle, 33″ × 22″, on the canvas, creating a 3″ border all around.

5. Cut the lime green fabric to 33″ × 22″. (Save scraps for bat eyes.)

6. Decoupage the green fabric to the entire area inside the borders, carefully smoothing out all wrinkles and bubbles.

7. Trace around the poster-board spiderweb pattern pieces onto the wrong side of the black fabric. (Be sure to save room for the cat.) Make sure that you are tracing on the wrong side of the fabric and that the pattern pieces are right side down.

TIP

The spiderweb sections are awkward to handle. Try applying a bit of gluestick to the web sections to help keep them in place while tracing.

8. Cut out the spiderweb pieces, and keep patterns and cut fabric together for identification until spiderweb segments have been put down onto the green background. Decoupage the spiderweb into place.

9. Place the letter pattern pieces face down on the back of the black with orange dot (Boo) fabric. Trace around each letter, tracing the **B** (in reverse) once and the **O** twice. Cut out the letters and decoupage into place, carefully smoothing out all wrinkles and bubbles.

10. With small, sharp scissors cut out the cat face details from the pattern. With the right side of the pattern facing the wrong side of the fabric, trace the cat body outline and details onto the black fabric. Cut out.

TIP

For the cat's eyes, use a hole punch to make the 2 circles from a scrap of the black fabric.

Use a hole punch for eyes.

11. On the back of the tone-on-tone black fabric, trace and cut out 14 bats. Using a hole punch and lime green scraps, make 28 circles for bats' eyes. Decoupage the bats' eyes into place.

12. Cut 2 border strips 4″ x 39, and 2 border strips 4″ x 30″ from the orange fabric with black dots.

13. Follow the instructions in Applying Borders (page 11).

14. Cut a 2″ x $1/4$″ strip of black fabric for the spider's suspension string.

15. Trace the spider onto the back of the purple fabric, and cut it out. Decoupage the suspension string and spider into place.

16. Referring to the photo on page 46, position and decoupage bats onto the border. Their heads should be approximately ½″ from the edge of the floorquilt and their wings approximately ½″ from the next bat's wings.

17. Referring to the floorquilt photo for placement (page 46), decoupage the cat into place.

18. Follow the instructions in Applying Protective Coatings & Backing (page 14).

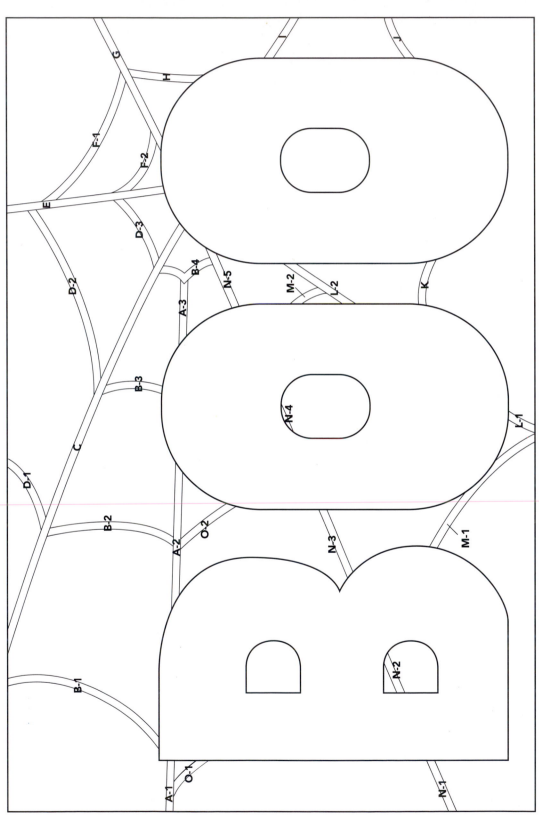

Enlarge pattern 400%.

Full-size pattern

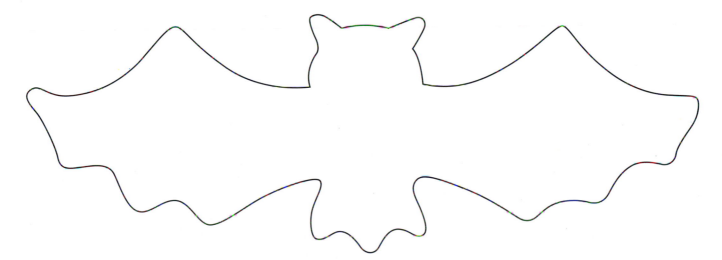

Full-size pattern

Enlarge pattern 125%

Dog Bone Dish Mat

Finished floorquilt: 18″ × 14″

Materials

- Basic tools and materials (page 7)
- Transparent template plastic, 1 sheet (12″ × 18″)
- Dark permanent marker
- Heavy cardstock, 1 sheet (8″ × 10″)
- Treated canvas (page 10) cut to 18″ × 14″
- Treated fabrics (page 8):
  1 fat quarter for background (or a 12″ × 8″ piece)
  ¼ yard fabric for left dog
  ¼ yard fabric for right dog
  ½ yard black fabric for outlines
  ¼ yard fabric for bones
  ½ yard fabric for outer border*

- Transparent drop cloth or acetate, 8″ × 10″

If you want an inner border and an outer border, as shown on the dish mat on page 53, you will need ¼ yard of fabric for the inner border and ¼ yard for the outer border.

Construction

1. Trace the patterns for the left dog and bone from page 54. Transfer all letter and number labels onto the patterns. Make patterns for the right dog by tracing the left dog again, flipping the tracing over, and darkening the lines with a marker.

2. Trace the bone onto transparent template plastic, and cut it out.

3. Trace each part of the left dog onto the template plastic, carefully labeling pieces (for example, **L Dog: L Ear** or **L3**), and cut out.

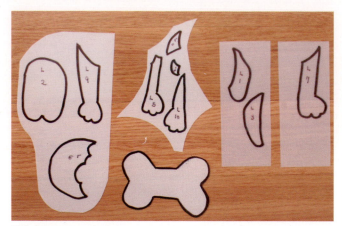

Make plastic templates.

Arrange and tape dog together.

NOTE

Labeling the templates is necessary because the left dog templates are flipped for the right dog.

4. Make an eye and a nose template. (The templates are the same for both right and left dogs.)

5. Trace all of the left dog's parts, except the chest, onto cardstock, leaving at least $1/2''$ between parts. Pencil a second line approximately $1/8''$ outside the traced line to make the outline patterns.

6. Label all of these templates with the same wording you used on the plastic templates, adding the word **Outline** to each one. Example: **L Dog: L Ear Outline** or **L3 Outline**. Cut out the outline templates.

7. Turn each template over, and label each for the right dog.

8. Place the plastic templates left side down on the wrong side of the appropriate left dog fabrics. Place the cardstock outline templates left side down on the wrong side of the black fabric. Trace and cut out all left dog parts and all left dog outlines. Trace and cut out 4 eyes and 2 noses from the black fabric. Consulting the photo, decoupage all parts and their corresponding outlines together. Trim extra outlines where they are not needed: where the ear meets the head, the underside of the chest, between the legs, at the tail, and at the chin. Let dry.

9. Working on top of the original tracing covered by a transparent drop cloth or acetate, use decoupage medium to arrange the left dog's outlined parts. Hold the assembled left dog together with masking tape so it can be moved as a single piece onto the background.

10. Flip the templates, and follow the same procedure for assembling the right dog, using the back of the copy that was darkened with the marker.

TIP

Adjusting the tilt of the head or conveying different body language can give each dog a unique personality.

11. Follow the same procedure to make 12 bones and 12 bone outlines.

NOTE

The bones are not symmetrical. This gives them a more realistic look.

12. Cut border fabric: 2 pieces $4'' \times 18''$ and 2 pieces $4'' \times 16''$.

For the dog mat with 2 borders, cut fabrics as follows:

Inner border:	Outer border:
2 pieces $2\frac{1}{2}'' \times 17''$	2 pieces $1\frac{1}{2}'' \times 18''$
2 pieces $2\frac{1}{2}'' \times 13''$	2 pieces $1\frac{1}{2}'' \times 16''$

13. Draw a centered rectangle 12″ × 8″ on the treated canvas, creating a 3″ border all around.

14. Cut the central design area background piece to 12″ × 8″ and decoupage it into place, carefully smoothing out all bubbles and wrinkles. Let dry.

15. Follow the instructions in Applying Borders (page 11). For double borders, apply inner borders as strips next to central design area and apply outer borders according to page 11.

16. To position the 2 dogs, locate the exact midpoint of the central design area, and mark it along the top and bottom with a piece of masking tape.

17. Place the left dog and the right dog side by side, equidistant from an imaginary centerline and 1″ above the edge of the lower border. Carefully remove the tape and decoupage the dogs into place.

18. Referring to the pattern and the photo, decoupage the noses and eyes into place. Decoupage the bones into place on the borders. Because the bones are not symmetrical, their placement can be rather casual. Dry thoroughly.

19. Follow the instructions in Applying Protective Coatings & Backing (page 14) to complete your dog's floorquilt.

TIP

This floorquilt is perfect as a mat under a dog's dish, but be sure to clean it as often as you do the kitchen floor. Reapply the paste wax (page 15) every 3 months to keep it thoroughly protected.

Doggie Dish Mat with 2 borders

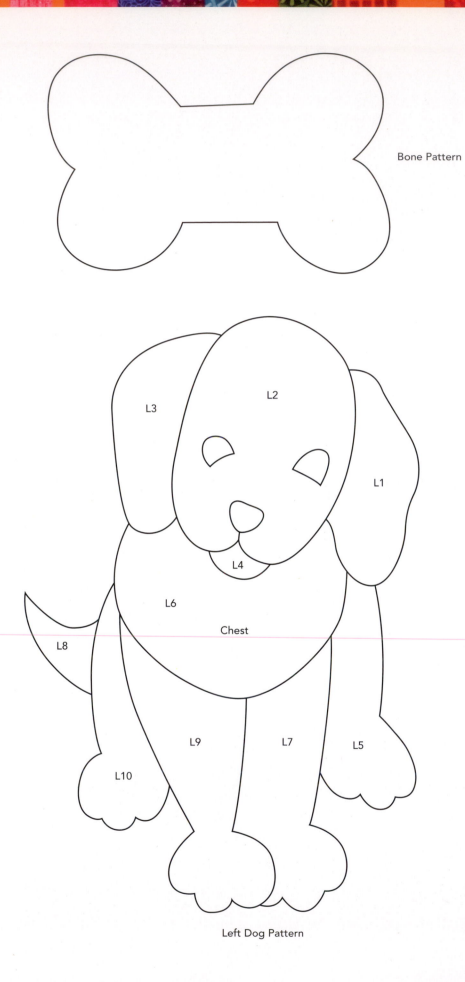

Bone Pattern

L3

L2

L1

L4

L6

Chest

L8

L9

L7

L5

L10

Left Dog Pattern

Good Kitty Cat Mat

Finished floorquilt: 18″ × 14″

Materials

- Basic tools and materials (page 7)
- Treated canvas (page 10) cut to 18″ × 14″
- White copy paper—2 sheets
- Transparent template plastic—1 sheet, 18″ × 22″
- Dark permanent marker
- Gluestick
- Treated fabrics (page 8):
  1 fat quarter for background (or a 14″ × 10″ piece)
  ¼ yard for right cat
  ¼ yard for left cat
  ⅜ yard for border
  ½ yard for dark outlines and letters
- Transparent drop cloth or acetate—1 piece, 8″ × 10″
- Transfer paper

TIP

Even though the blue outline worked to define the red cat, there was not quite enough contrast in the border for the blue letters to be read easily. Dark blue permanent marker to the rescue! This is not cheating, because there are no rules in floorquilting except to enjoy the process and the result.

Construction

1. Trace and label the right cat placement guide from page 58 onto white copy paper, using the black outlines. Make 2 copies. Enhance the lines on the reverse side of 1 copy with a dark permanent marker. Label this side **Left Cat Outlines.**

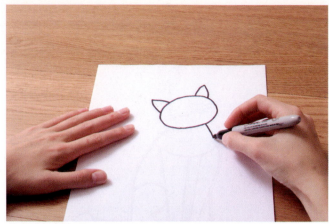

Trace the placement guide.

2. Use the dark marker to trace the patterns drawn in red on page 60 for the right cat parts onto transparent template plastic. Carefully cut them out.

3. Label each plastic template with a dark permanent marker. For example, **R1 = Right Cat: Part 1**.

4. Turn the templates over, and label them for the left cat. For example, **L1 = Left Cat: Part 1**. Adhere pieces of masking tape to the reverse side and write the labels on the tape, if you prefer.

5. Make templates for the outline pieces from Step 1 in the same manner. Label each template as you did before. For example, **R1 Outline = Right Cat: Part 1 Outline.**

6. Turn the templates over, and label the parts for the left cat. For example, **L1 Outline = Left Cat: Part 1 Outline**.

7. Make templates for the facial features and whiskers (page 60) and for the letters that you'll need. Use the alphabet pattern on page 59.

8. Assemble all the templates for the parts of the right cat. Set aside the outline templates.

9. Trace and cut out 5 sets of the words *Good Kitty* (or choose your own words and letters). Cut 2 sets of facial features from the outline fabric. You'll need a total of 12 whiskers.

10. Place the right cat templates face down on the back of the right cat fabric (ignore the **L** labels). If necessary, use a gluestick to hold the templates in place. Trace around the templates with a pencil.

11. Cut out each part, and label it with a bit of masking tape placed on the **front** of the piece.

12. Follow the same process to cut and label the outline pieces for the right cat using the dark fabric.

13. Place all right cat parts onto the corresponding right outline pieces. Decoupage into place, referring to the placement guide.

NOTE

The chest (7) has only 1 side outlined. The cat body (5) has a partial outline on 1 side. The ears, tail, and leg 1 use the outlines of the adjacent piece.

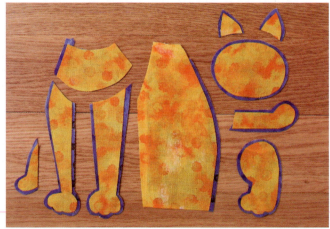

Decoupage parts onto outlines.

14. Use the placement guide to assemble the right cat by placing the paper guide under a piece of transparent drop cloth or acetate to keep it clean. Decoupage all of the right cat parts into place. Hold the ears and tail in place with masking tape. Let dry.

NOTE

Because Part 5 extends from the body up behind the head, almost all of the cat can be preassembled and easily moved into place later.

Decoupage right cat parts into place.

15. Turn all the templates over to the left cat side, and separate the cat and outline templates.

16. Repeat Steps 10 through 14 to cut and assemble the left cat. Let dry.

17. Cut the background fabric to 14″ × 10″.

18. Cut border fabrics: 2 strips, 3″ × 18″, and 2 strips, 3″ × 16″.

19. Draw a 14″ × 10″ rectangle on the canvas, creating a 2″ border on all sides.

20. Decoupage the background fabric in place on the canvas, carefully smoothing out any bubbles or wrinkles. Let dry.

21. Follow the instructions in Applying Borders (page 11).

TIP

During construction, it is often necessary to mark the front of a floorquilt for positioning a design or for keeping elements in line or evenly spaced. My favorite method is to put a piece of painter's masking tape at the required location and mark the tape, or use a strip of tape to provide a straight line. Remove the tape after it has served its purpose.

22. To position the cats, locate the exact midpoint of the central design area, and mark it along the top and bottom with a piece of masking tape. Place cats equidistant from the imaginary centerline and ½″ above the lower border. Remove any tape and decoupage the cats into place.

23. Apply the facial features to both cats.

24. Place the letters about ½″ from the outer edge. Adjust the positioning until you're satisfied; then decoupage into place. Let dry thoroughly.

TIP

It is helpful to use a transparent ruler or a ½″ strip of paper or tape along the outer edge to keep the letters straight.

25. Follow the instructions in Applying Protective Coatings and Backing (page 14).

Right Cat Placement Guide (Black = Outline; Red = Cat)

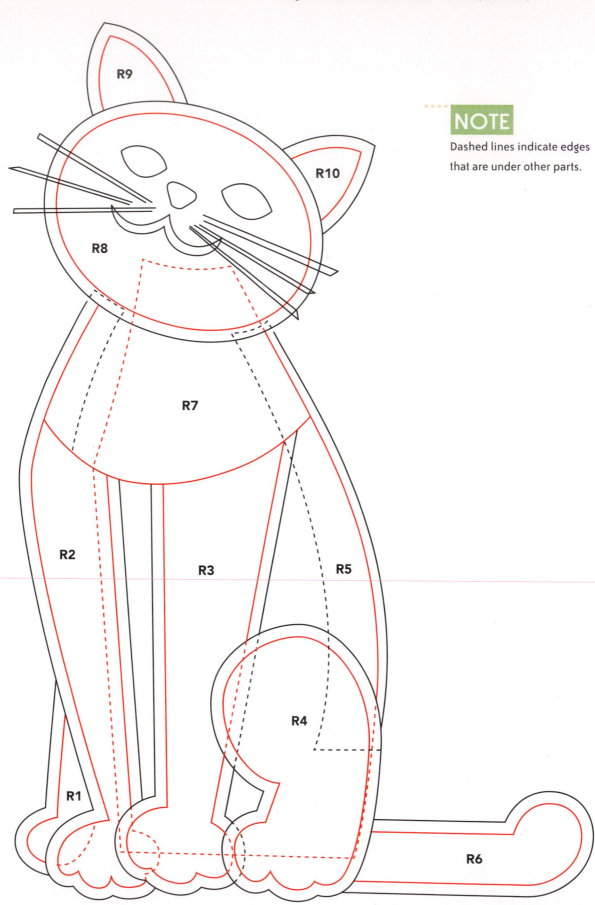

NOTE
Dashed lines indicate edges that are under other parts.

Alphabet

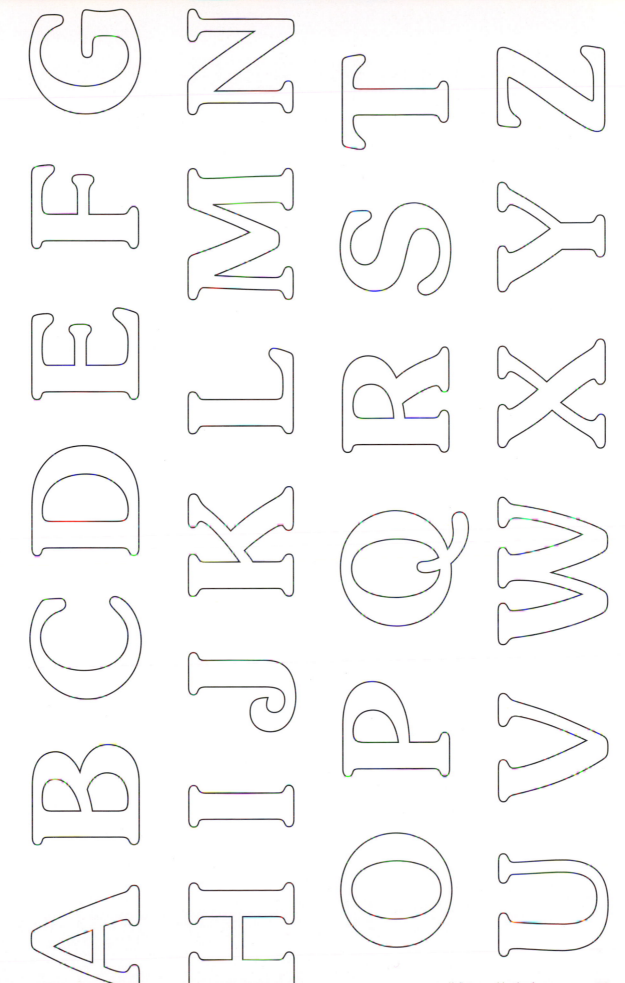

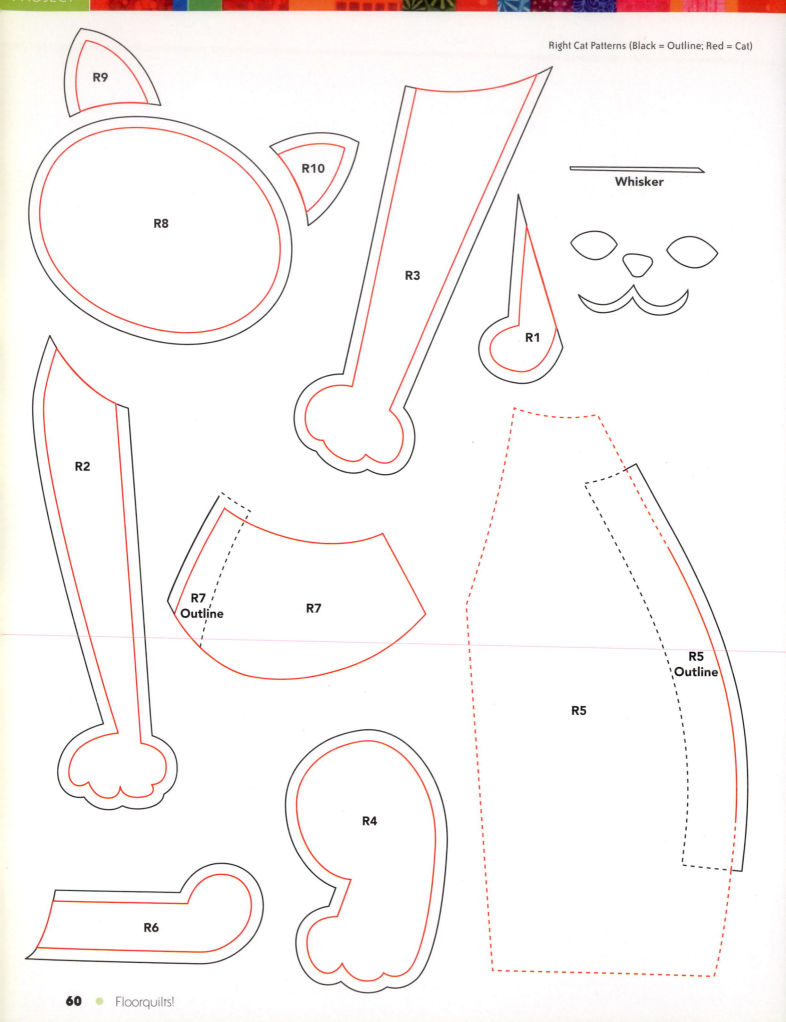

Right Cat Patterns (Black = Outline; Red = Cat)

R9

R10

R8

Whisker

R3

R1

R2

R7
Outline

R7

R5
Outline

R5

R4

R6

Off-the-Floorquilts

Have leftovers from previous projects? I love scraps! Here are several ways to use them. From creating coasters to brewing up a bookmark, no scrap is too small.

Reversible Coasters

Many of the floorquilt projects use $4\frac{1}{2}''$ squares, the perfect size for coasters. If you have leftover squares that are larger, simply cut them down.

Finished size: $4\frac{1}{2}'' \times 4\frac{1}{2}''$

Materials

Materials listed are for 1 coaster.

- Basic tools and materials (page 7)
- Treated canvas (page 10) cut to $4\frac{1}{2}'' \times 4\frac{1}{2}''$
- Treated fabrics (page 8):
  2 squares $4\frac{1}{2}'' \times 4\frac{1}{2}''$ (decorated from a previous project or plain)
  2 strips $1'' \times 4\frac{1}{2}''$
  2 strips $1'' \times 5\frac{1}{2}''$

Construction

1. Decoupage a $4\frac{1}{2}'' \times 4\frac{1}{2}''$ fabric square to the treated canvas, smoothing out all bubbles and wrinkles. Let dry.

2. Turn canvas over, and decoupage the other fabric square to that side. Smooth and let dry.

3. Fold the $1''$ strips of treated fabric in half lengthwise, creating a $\frac{1}{2}''$ border on each side. Follow the instructions in Applying Borders (page 11). Let dry.

4. Follow the instructions in Applying Protective Coatings (page 14).

TIP

Coasters used on highly polished surfaces can be decorated on the front and backed with cork (see Trivet construction, page 63).

Trivets

These trivets are splendid showcases for your design flair (read: showing off). Any of the designs featured in Squares Dancing (pages 16–27) should provide plenty of fuel for your imagination. Perhaps you already have leftovers from some of these projects. A set of a few trivets makes a practical gift with that "Wow! You made these for me?!" bonus.

Materials

Materials listed are for 1 trivet.

- Basic tools and materials (page 7)
- Treated canvas (page 10) cut to 6″ × 6″
- Treated fabrics (page 8):
  6″ square (decorated or plain)
  2 strips 1″ × 6″
  2 strips 1″ × 8″
- 5¾″ square of ¼″-thick cork

Construction

1. Decoupage the treated-fabric square to the treated canvas, and let dry.

2. Fold the 1″ strips lengthwise so that there is ½″ on each side. Follow the instructions in Applying Borders (page 11). Let dry.

3. Follow the instructions for Applying Protective Coatings (page 14).

4. Using full-strength decoupage medium, glue the cork to the underside of the trivet. Use a weight to hold the layers together until dry.

Finished size: 6″ × 6″

Serving Trays

Trays are an obvious surface for decorating with fabric decoupage. The tray in the center came from a thrift store. I painted it black and decorated it with treated fabrics, six Handkerchief Corners blocks (page 17) and a floral border to fill in the uneven spaces. Coat and seal following the Applying Protective Coatings instructions (page 14). All of the trays have performed admirably and often.

Finished size depends on size of premade tray.

The scalloped wooden trays found me at a going-out-of-business grocery store. Now they get a lot more attention with patchy geometric designs of squares and circles.

Reversible Placemats

These placemats are designed to use scraps from other projects. Choose a color scheme of three different colors; then have fun rummaging through your scraps to see how many you can use up.

Finished size: 17″ × 13″

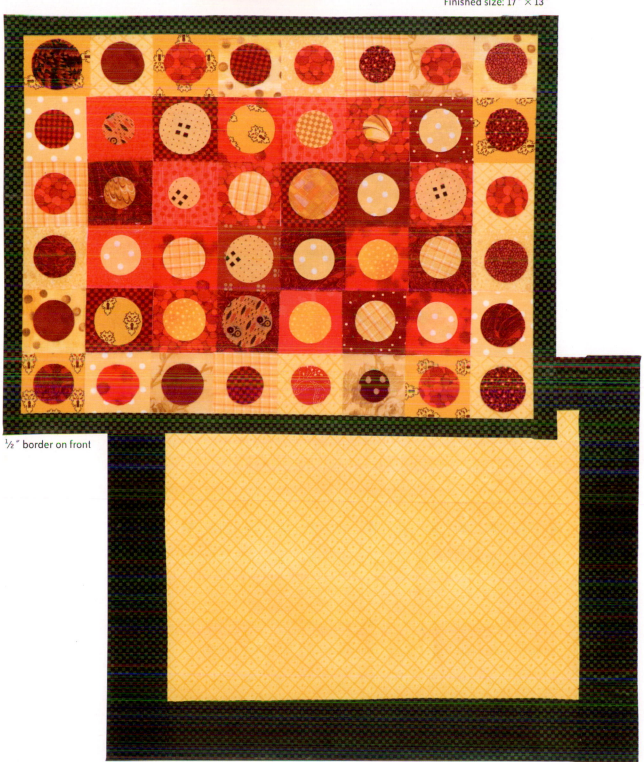

½″ border on front

2″ border on back

Materials

Materials listed are for 6 placemats.

- Basic tools and materials (page 7)
- Circle template (1¼" diameter) or circle cutter (Sources, page 78)
- Treated fabrics (page 8):
  1 yard total color A scraps
  1¼ yards color A fabric for the placemat backs
  1 yard total color B scraps
  1 yard color C for borders
  1¼ yards muslin (bleached or unbleached)

Construction

1. From the color A scraps:
Cut 144 squares 2" × 2".
Cut 144 circles 1¼" in diameter.

2. From the color A fabric:
Cut 6 pieces 17" × 13", for the backs of the placemats.

3. From the color B scraps:
Cut 144 squares 2" × 2".
Cut 144 circles 1¼" in diameter.

4. From the color C fabric:
Cut 12 border strips 2½" wide × 17" long.
Cut 12 border strips 2½" wide × 14" long.

5. From the muslin:
Cut 6 pieces 17" × 13".

6. Draw a ½" border all around on one side of each 17" × 13" piece of treated muslin.

7. Decoupage circles onto squares of the opposite color (color A circles on color B squares, and vice versa). Let dry.

8. Referring to the photo for placement, decoupage decorated squares onto the treated muslin. Let dry thoroughly.

9. Turn mats over, and decoupage the 17" × 13" pieces of color A to the backs of the placemats.

Decoupage fabric onto back of placemat.

Decoupage circles onto squares

10. Follow the instructions for Applying Borders (page 11), beginning on the decorated side. The finished placemats have a ½" border on the front and a 2" border on the back.

11. For both fronts and backs of all placemats, follow the instructions for Applying Protective Coatings (page 14). Because both sides of the placemats can be used, constantly make sure that there is no decoupage medium residue on either side as you are working.

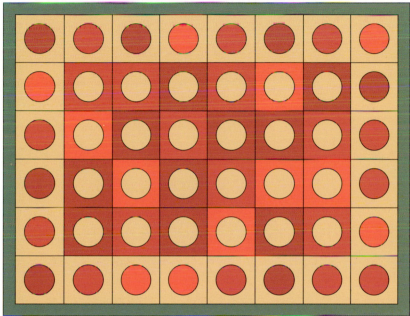

Front of placemat
Color A=Yellow, Color B=Red, Color C=Green

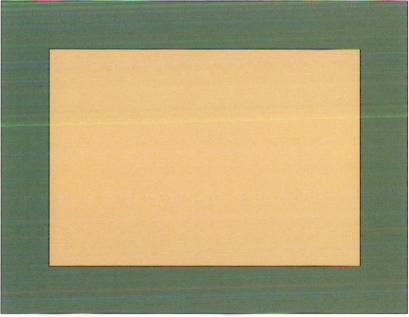

Reverse side of placemat

"That's My Bag!" Tags

Here's a way to make that black suitcase unmistakably yours. All it takes are these reversible tags, made of two bound layers of treated fabrics. You can make the tags any size that you wish.

Finished size: 2″ × 4″ or 4″ × 4″

Materials

Materials listed are for 1 tag.

- Basic tools and materials (page 7)
- Treated fabrics (page 8):
  2 squares 4″ × 4″ or 2 rectangles 2″ × 4″
  1″ strips 4″ and 6″ long, for borders
  Scraps for adding designs
- Hole punch or nail
- Ribbon

Construction

1. Decorate one or both pieces of treated fabric (squares or rectangles) using other treated fabric scraps; apply with decoupage medium.

Decoupage designs on squares.

2. Decoupage the 2 pieces together, right sides out. Let dry.

Decoupage squares together.

3. Cut 2 border strips the same length as the 2 longer sides, and 2 border strips that are 2″ longer than the 2 shorter sides.

4. Follow instructions for Applying Borders (page 11) to create a ½″ border on each side of the tag.

Add borders.

5. Follow the instructions for Applying Protective Coatings (page 14) to both sides.

6. Use a nail or punch to make a hole in one corner for the ribbon. Thread the ribbon through the hole, and tie it.

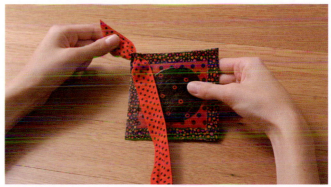

Add a ribbon tie.

7. Now that you're not searching the luggage carousel for your bags, enjoy your added vacation time!

Bookmarks

These great fish from my fabric stash show up here adorning bookmarks that are simply made of two treated fabrics, bound, coated, and sealed back to back. This project is proof positive that one should never throw any fabric away!

TIP

Cutting out the fish was easy because they were printed on a black background. Leaving a small black border provided an outline and hid any fussy-cutting inaccuracies.

Finished size: 4˝ to 7˝

These inquisitive bookworms are also seen on the *Butterflies & Vines* floorquilt, page 43.

TIP

Resist humility. Always accept compliments graciously ("Thank you so much" is just fine!), and never point out mistakes.

Gallery

Even though the process of making a floorquilt is easier than quiltmaking, it provides the same sense of satisfaction that comes from combining designs and colors of fabrics to create beauty you can live with.

All artwork is by the author unless indicated.

Students' floorquilts, photo by Parsley Steinweiss

Fassetts of Summer, by Hilary Ward

Photo by Tom Young

Random Compliments

Photo by Tom Young

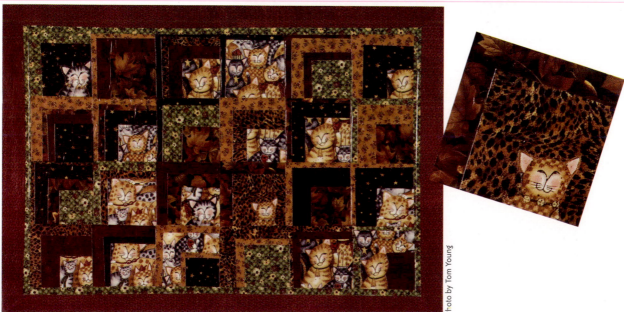

Kitty Corners

Photo by Tom Young

Mighty Busy Miters

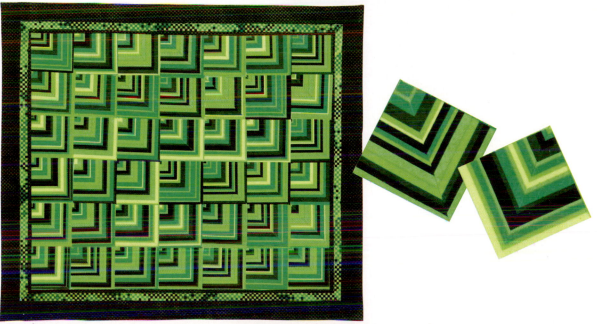

Mitered Green Zones

Accessories Underfoot

Photo by Tom Young

Kornering Kaffe Fassett & Friends

Kitchen's Bouquet

Serendipitous Stripes

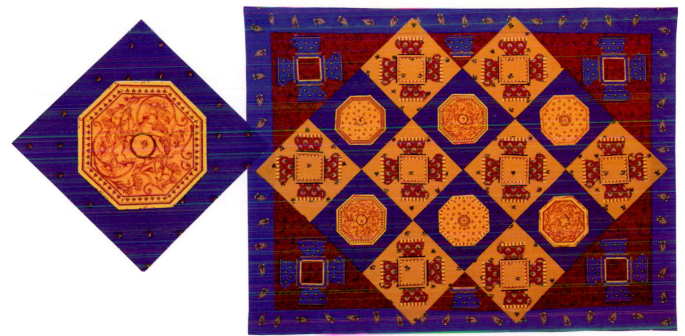

Coffee & Dessert

Photo by Tom Young

Running Rabbits

Photo by Tom Young

Apron Boutique

90 Degrees of Patriotism

Photo by Tom Young

Placemat: Side 1

Placemat: Side 2

About the Author

Photo by Tom Young

She has a textile radar that just about affects her heart rate when she sees a wonderful piece of art or craft created with fabric.

Since the ubiquitous textile design experience of weaving pot holders on a square metal loom using stretchy cotton loops, Ellen has been hooked on the broad medium of textiles. Working on or with fabrics has always had a gravitational pull on her life. Girl Scouts in her small, southern hometown provided useful skills, such as righting a flipped canoe, pitching a tent, making s'mores (of course), and especially needlework.

Ellen has studied and designed professionally in many branches of needlework, from needlepoint to appliqué to embroidery and quilting. She has a textile radar that just about affects her heart rate when she sees a wonderful piece of art or craft created with fabric. Whether going to London and studying exquisite crewelwork at the Victoria and Albert Museum or sitting in church behind Virginia Avery and studying her joyous wearable art, Ellen is inspired and happy to see art and skill combined in a medium that speaks her language.

Ellen created the idea of floorquilts to solve a problem. The question was how her love of well-designed textiles on the floor could coexist with her love of dogs in various stages of development (chewing rug corners being one of the stages). Floorquilts became the solution.

When she's not giving lessons at the Quilt Cottage in Mamaroneck, Ellen lives in Rye, New York, with her husband, Mitch, and their two dogs, Broadway and Charlie. Ellen and her family, human and otherwise, hope that making and living with floorquilts will give you and your family many reasons to smile.

Photo by Mike Henes

Broadway and Charlie

Sources

Supplies

3-in-1 Color Tool
Choose or match colors with confidence!
For more fine books, ask for a free catalog.

C&T Publishing
P.O. Box 1456
Lafayette, CA 94549
(800) 284-1114
www.ctpub.com

C&T Publishing's professional photography services are now available to the public. Visit us at www.ctmediaservices.com.

Floorquilt Essentials Supply Kit
Materials for making a 36″ × 24″ project, except the fabric!
Includes canvas, gesso, Mod Podge, Polycrylic, Saf-T-Bak,
Skid-Tex, and sponge brushes.

Quilt Cottage Kits
414 Mamaroneck Avenue
Mamaroneck, NY 10543
(914) 777-1333
www.quiltcottage.net

Fredrix Acrylic-Primed Artist Canvas
Choose Dixie—Style 123: very heavy weight
100% cotton duck.

Tara Materials, Inc.
P.O. Box 646
Lawrenceville, GA 30046
www.taramaterials.com or www.fredrixartistcanvas.com

Gesso
Gesso is available at any good art supply store
(high quality is not required).

Mod Podge—Matte
This is a water-based decoupage medium and sealer.

Plaid Enterprises
3225 Westech Drive
Norcross, GA 30092
(800) 842-4197
www.plaidonline.com

Polycrylic and Clear Paste Finishing Wax
Minwax Company
10 Mountainview Road
Upper Saddle River, NJ 07458
(800) 523-9299
www.minwax.com

Butcher's Wax (or *Bowling Alley Paste Wax*)
BWC Company
(800) 569-0394
www.bwccompany.com

Template Plastic
Nonslip vinyl template sheets

W. H. Collins, Inc.
Spartenburg, SC 29304

No-Melt Mylar Template Plastic
Wrights—EZ Quilting
P.O. Box 398
West Warren, MA 01092
(800) 660-0415
www.wrights.com

Saral Wax-Free Transfer Paper
Send a SASE to the Free Sample Department
for a sample.

Saral Paper Corporation
400 East 55th Street, Suite 14C
New York, NY 10022
(212) 223-3322
www.saralpaper.com

Saf-T-Bak Rug-Backing Compound
This product is often sold with supplies for rug hooking.

Testworth Laboratories, Inc.
P.O. Box 91
Columbia City, IN 46725
(219) 244-5137

Bondex Skid-Tex
This nonskid additive for paint is available at most
paint stores.

Zinsser Company, Inc.
173 Belmont Drive
Somerset, NJ 08875
(732) 469-8100
www.zinsser.com

Circle Cutter

Fiskars Brands, Inc.
School, Office & Craft Division
2537 Daniels St.
Madison, WI 53718
(866) 348-5661
www.fiskars.com

Olfa Rotary Cutter and Self-Healing Mat

OLFA—North America
5500 North Pearl Street, Suite 400
Rosemont, IL 60018
(800) 962-OLFA
www.olfa.com

Omnigrid Heavy Plastic Gridded Ruler

Dritz Company
950 Brisack Road
Spartansburg, SC 29303
(803) 587-5212
www.dritz.com

Rug Grip Rug Padding

Capel Inc.
P.O. Box 826
Troy, NC 27371
www.capelrugs.com

Lightweight Fusible Interfacing

Pellon Consumer Products
3440 Industrial Drive
Durham, NC 27704
(770) 491-8001 x2986
www.shoppellon.com

Fabrics

Many of the fabrics used to create the floorquilts in this book are no longer available because of the lengthy time between creating projects and the book's publication. However, these manufacturers consistently produce high-quality fabrics of good design. By the time you're shopping for fabrics for your first floorquilt, the selection will be wider and even better!

Robert Kaufman Fabrics

129 West 132nd Street
Los Angeles, CA 90061
(800) 877-2066
www.robertkaufman.com

M & S Textiles

136 Cromwell Street
Collingwood, Melbourne
VIC 3066 Australia
+61-03-9417-0052

Marjorie Lee Bevis Marbled Fabrics & Accessories

1401 Oakwood Drive
Oakland, OR 97462
(541) 459-1921
www.marbledfabrics.com

Kaffe Fassett for Westminster Fabrics

4 Townsend Avenue—Unit 8
Nashua, NH 03063
www.kaffefassett.com

Timeless Treasures Fabrics

483 Broadway
New York, NY 10013
(212) 226-1400
www.ttfabrics.com

FreeSpirit Fabrics

c/o Westminster Fibers, Inc.
3430 Toringdon Way—Suite 301
Charlotte, NC 28277
(704) 329-5822

Cotton Patch

1025 Brown Ave.
Lafayette, CA 94549
(800) 835-4418
www.quiltusa.com

Great Titles
from

C&T PUBLISHING

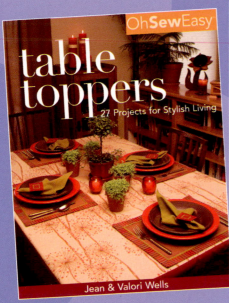

Available at your local retailer or
www.ctpub.com or **800.284.1114**